Crushed to Sparkle

HOW TO POSITIVELY BUILD YOURSELF UP FROM A BROKEN RELATIONSHIP

This includes relationships

With a Partner, Family or Friends, and even business associates or corporate organisations;
And other institutions

Anyone and Anything
That has made you feel inadequate.

Juliyah Brown

Foreword by Award winning author
Vishal Morjaria

www.crushedtosparkle.com

Crushed to Sparkle

First Edition Published by Juliyah Brown
www.crushedtosparkle.com

Copyright © 2020 Juliyah Brown

WOW Book Publishing™

ISBN: 9798668537235

Warning—Disclaimer

The purpose of this book is to educate and entertain.
The author and/or publisher do not guarantee that anyone
following these techniques, suggestions, tips, ideas, or
strategies will become successful. The author and/or
publisher shall have neither liability nor responsibility
to anyone with respect to any loss or damage caused,
or alleged to be caused, directly or indirectly by the
information contained in this book.

Table of Contents

About the Author V

Acknowledgements IX

Foreword XV

Why read this book and how will it help you? XVII

How to use this book XXIII

Chapter 1
Breakdown 29

Chapter 2
Build Up 47

Chapter 3
Breakthrough 65

Chapter 4
Break Free 83

Chapter 5
FAST TRACK to Self-Discovery:
"Being a Brand-New Me" 115

Chapter 6
FAST TRACK: Food for Thought on Broken
Relationships Case studies 123

Chapter 7
FAST TRACK: Are you a Carer?...................143

Chapter 8
FAST TRACK: Facing Procrastination.....................155

Chapter 9
Bonus Gift: Facing the Challenge of Letting Go 161

Chapter 10
Bonus Gift: Summary Les Brown Speaks
on Getting UNSTUCK..................................167

Chapter 11
JULIYAH'S "MAGIC" KEYS............................177

Chapter 12
Extra Boosters For You!................................183

VIP PRAYERS..187

About the Author

Juliyah Brown is an author, teacher, trainer, trader, lifestyle Coach, and a professional motivational and inspirational public speaker. She has a Master's degree graduating with a distinction.

She has set up social enterprise hubs for micro businesses, professional education training, learning and community development. Juliyah has set up her own business—Queen Angel Creations (**www.queenangelcreations.com**)—with the mantra: **"Gift a piece of happiness"** that creates bespoke gifts from birth all the way through death.

Juliyah, has also set up Gold Mine Mind Training Services Limited (**www.Goldminemind.com**): with the mantra: **"I SEE, I RISE UP!! I BUILD!!!"**, which focuses on lifestyle management and empowers people to create the life that they desire and deserve to live.

Juliyah's recent collaboration and joint business venture is called Naked Truth Diamonds, with the mantra: **"You are amazing"**, which supports, facilitates and empowers highly stressed city workers to find more harmony in their life.

Juliyah is passionate about helping people to become the best they can be. She is fun, fair and firm; she lays bare many ways of decluttering, streamlining and bringing clarity to life.

Juliyah loves life; she teaches honestly, coaches ethically, mentors deeply and trains others to release and realise their gifts of goodness and greatness in a mindful manner. She proactively, upon meeting new people, looks to connect with them at their place of need.

Juliyah wrote this **self discovery, healing, journey journal**, as a toolkit guide, to empower you through several key principles that will enable you to discover the best version of yourself.

This toolkit is based on real life challenges and the need to find solutions, as Juliyah firmly believes, where there is will there is a way — your way.

Juliyah Brown, frequently writes, speaks, guides, facilitates, leads, motivates and coaches people. Juliyah, aims to help people, by positively building themselves up from **broken relationships with: family members,**

About the Author

friends, work colleagues, bosses, partners, training and educational establishments, organisations etc.

To understand more about finding yourself through self-discovery go to:

www.CrushedtoSparkle.com

For more of Juliyah's: insights, workshops, regular e-articles, books, blogs, podcasts, videos and retreats. Or if you would like to book her for speaking engagements at your next event, kindly email:

Juliyah@CrushedtoSparkle.com

Thank you.
Juliyah aka Queen Angel xxx

Acknowledgements

This book would not have been made possible without the help and encouragement of many people.

My deepest gratitude goes out to God, the Most High, who allowed me to be here today. Thank you, Lord, infinite source of energy and intelligence.

My positive ancestors
[Inspirational, Beloved]

I genuinely wish to thank my son, my wonderful and amazing son: **King "Champion" Leeshaun Xavier Brown**, who watched his mother go through so much as he was growing up, and he has developed into a well-rounded, loving, kind, joyful, caring and purposeful, handsome young ambitious man, who now wishes to enter into the world of International Relations and is looking to make positive world changes. Leeshaun, I would not have been able to achieve this incredible opportunity without your love, time, support, interest and peace of mind. Leeshaun, you are a blessing and you are blessed.

I would love to thank my powerful mother, so loving and supportive, **Queen Mother Nora, (Nal, Blossom)**

Brown, a loving and caring nurse, who was a prolific social networker, the forerunner to social media! Through all the sacrifices that she made to ensure that ALL of her children were able to pursue their dreams. Also, to **my late father Joseph Nathaniel Brown**, a master carpenter, cabinet maker and body builder for his strength of character, his indomitable spirit to focus and move forward and also being able to follow through on his dreams.

To my **late, great Godmother, Mabel James**, as well as to my living Godmother **Lorraine Russell**, who is strong, powerful and very direct in her outlook on life.

I would love to say amazing thanks to **Aunty Polly (Joan),** who has been a real powerhouse of hope, a rock, a guiding light and a tower of strength when times were so bleak. You truly are a remarkable, loving, patient, caring, resourceful and so supportive towards my mother's health and welfare and my wellbeing. you are a phenomenal woman. Thank you, Aunty Polly, for also introducing me to an amazing, caring and outstanding lady, **Joan K.**

To **my amazing queens**, my baby **Queen Angel**, Queen Ocean, **Janice** Queen **Sophia**, Queen **Joi**, Queen **Annette** and Queen **Andrea**.

Acknowledgements

To **my mighty kings, Tony Rose** a cousin, so much like a brother to me, and **Mimoune, Mimz,** for showing good vibrations of pure innocent love from across the seas. **Master Noel Blackman, "Mr Tae Kwon Do,"** who over the years has became like a second father to me, and who is now Lee's Godfather. To **Sam**, Lee's 2nd Godfather, for being, truly family and community focused. Sam is so highly intellectually gifted and a fountain of knowledge, he is genuinely solutions oriented when things appeared dire. Sam is always helping the voiceless to be heard.

To my late brothers: **Erroll Powell and Bunny Scarlett** and my living and loving, strong brother **Warren Scarlett** and to all my upcoming enterprising, entrepreneurial nieces and nephews. Believe in yourselves and aim higher than high!

Thank you, **Cousin Dave**, you showed me how hard work and focus can pay off, you have never forgotten my mother and have always been there for her. Thank you, to your amazing sister, **Cousin Dianna**, Dianna, you have been a true earth angel helping me to take care of mum, you genuinely have a loving family oriented heart. And finally to your awesome mother, **Aunty Pauline**, Aunty Pauline, although you were across the Atlantic seas, you were a mighty strong tower of strength providing a guiding light of wisdom and action, when things were most challenging for me, you came as a Mother Earth Angel, to help mum and I get through.

Thank you to my amazing **sisters-in-law:** Angela, Hazel, Yvette, Pauline, Audrey, Maureen, Mackeba and Rasheeda

I am acknowledging the **departed souls of:** Queen Mother Nana Yaa Asantewa, Chevalier de St George, Harriet Tubman, Marcus Garvey, Bob Marley, Martin Luther King, Malcolm X, Muhammad Ali, Princess Diana, Mother Teresa, Nelson Mandela, Steve Jobs, James Brown, Aretha Franklin, Mayo Angelou, Michal Jackson, Whitney Houston, Prince and Bruce Lee and so many other endless greats, who have shown love unconditionally, with inclusivity, equality and diversity to humanity despite social and media injustices.

I am grateful for the leadership of the Queen, President Barak Obama, First Lady Michelle Obama, Oprah Winfrey, Prince William and Kate, Prince Harry and Meghan, and many others whom I have not named but who continue to tirelessly help make the world a better place for you and for me.

I would like to acknowledge all those involved in **spiritual work,** with special thanks to: St Andrew's Church, Burnt Oak Christian Fellowship, Willesden

Acknowledgements

New Testament Church, Harrow Apostolic Church, Holy Ghost Power Chapel (Edgware, South Harrow) Brahma Kumaris World Spiritual University, KICC, V2V, UKCG, Prince Ministries, Deepak ChopraThe Potter's House, Joel Olsteen, for the spiritual work they are doing in uplifting individuals, families, organisations, communities, societies and humanity.

I would like to acknowledge some of the great business and influential minds that I have had the pleasure of learning from and also the pleasure of meeting such as: Les Brown, Vishal Morjaria, Mary J. Blige, Bishop TD Jakes, Brian Tracey, Michael Tracey, Bianca Miller & Byron Cole, Joyce Meyers, Abraham Hicks, Louise Hay, Naomi Campbell, Robert Kiyosaki, David Imonitie, Bob Proctor, Christopher Terry, Isis De La Torre, Seth Bernstein, Tony Robbins, Emma Jones (MBE) Warren Buffet, Zig Ziglar, Jim Rohn, Mac Attram, Gerry Robert, Minister Louis Farrakhan, Andy Harrington, Dr Stephen Ssali, James Nicholson, Chuck D, T Harv Erker, Marcus De Maria, Destiny's Child, Kirk Franklin, Yolanda Adams, Common, Creflo Dollar, KRS-1, Zain Ahmed, Mark Simpson and Levi Roots.

To all of the following: clients, fellow carers, fellow teachers, friends, work colleagues, business associates, students, family members who believed in me.

Collectively, you have shown me how much a book like this one was so critically needed.

Unusually, I would like to thank all of those people and organisations who went out of their way to attempt to crush me. **These people pretended** to be my 'friends' or 'business associates', my 'soul life partners'. A number of educational, council and LPA bodies systematically looked to weaken my spirit. However, the cruellest, calculated attacks were from my "closest blood family members," who strategically and relentlessly plotted for my downfall.

What you thought was bad, turned out good for me, through God's love, grace and mercy. I am not bitter, I am better, more focussed. I have forgiven, let go of and moved on to a bigger brighter future of givers gain.

I am now operating from a place and space of peace, joy and abundance.

Ironically, the drama and emotional trauma you attempted to put me under actually provided the substance to create this book which will help others to shine, RISE UP! STAY UP! MOVE UP!

Thank you.
Juliyah aka Queen Angel xxx

Foreword

Juliyah, has been most industrious to capture a collection of her own life experiences and that of so many others into such a proactive and captivating book.

This is an extraordinary book which enables the reader to write and create their own history whilst reading.

This self-discovery toolkit also includes useful quotes from a variety of learned sources which triggers personal reflection and creates a deeper and more meaningful inner connection.

This journal is creatively put together in five parts:

1. Four Pillars
2. Fast track to self-discovery
3. Bonus gifts
4. Juliyah's Magic keys
5. VIP

Juliyah's style is so conversational that you feel she is literally speaking to you personally right off the page.

Crushed to Sparkle

Juliyah feels extremely passionate about giving readers the tools they need to live the life that they desire and deserve.

This book should be on your bookshelf or in your bookcase and I believe it should be read at least once a year so you can see your life history unfolding and your own story organically evolving.

Vishal Morjaria
Award Winning Author and
International Speaker

Why read this book and how will it help you?

Your Journey to an extraordinary life

This is no ordinary book just as you are no ordinary person! This book has the secret to create an extraordinary life for you, if you are open to change your way of thinking and doing things. It will require you to extend your thinking beyond your physical being into connecting with your spiritual being, one that radiates with divine energy.

Therefore, if you are ready to apply and implement what is being shared within this self-discovery healing toolkit, it will become a journey where you will meet your future self NOW! As a result, your future self will thank you for it.

This book will transform your life, only if you are willing to be open to change. Listen, please do not take my word for it, read this book for yourself and leave scepticism, criticism and doubt out for 21 days, OK?

Detox your mind of negative thoughts, flush them out immediately, and allow good wholesome positive thoughts to fill that empty space, which is now a clear space, to bathe, clean and clear your mind, body, and soul. After all, you mind is fertile, so do not let other's dirty feet tamper, trample or stamp on your mind!

Please work on creating and sustaining a positive mindset. Be aggressive to live in the positive zone. Remove yourself from dream stealers, dream catchers, criticizers, naysayers. Remove yourself from those who only doubt everything and anything you do.

Detox and Declutter

My dear friend, you need to detox; you need to declutter. You need to question who and what is surrounding you. Take an honest look at your home, family, friends, work colleagues, business associates, place of worship and fellowship. Please answer this question: "**Who really is there for you in both the good and the bad times?**" It is time to cut yourself off from things and people, as time waits for no one. If these people are not helping or nourishing you, then spend less time with them or choose to no longer interact or engage in their presence, as you are a present, a gift, a beautiful gift to the world, you truly are.

Maybe, just maybe, if you took time seriously, you would not be wasting it on meaningless things that do not add value to your life. Such activities are relentless distractions that will rob your life time away!

Improving the quality of your life

So now let us look at how you can improve the quality of your life, right here, right now. It all begins with a new way of thinking; remember, what you focus on intensifies, expands, and magnifies. So, I ask you to think positively as often as you can, as you do want good things to manifest in your life, don't you?

Change your thinking and change your life, through this journal of self-discovery, you will **move from stagnation to transformation.** So, turn the page slowly and let us begin exploring **the wonderful story of you.**

Please make it a habit NOW to replace worry, anxiety and other negative thoughts, with empowering, uplifting, nourishing and positive thoughts to move your life forward and upwards!

Please be informed that most of these negative thoughts may never happen, yet they have robbed you of years of your life!!!

Stop wasting your time, stop being a prisoner trapped in the past, by passing the present and wishing for a better future — really?? Come on, wake up!

You are alive NOW, live NOW, the past has gone!, This is YOUR moment, this is YOUR time, be present, command your presence! Be fully in this present time zone, as the decisions you make or not make will define your tomorrows!!!!

Sorry, I just had to preach, teach, reach and connect with you!!! Look, somehow, one day, you have to wake up out of your slumber, get energised, wakey, wakey, **RISE UP, GET UP, STAND UP, STAY UP, MOVE UP** and don't give up the good fight of being the best version of yourself!!!

MOVE UP, STEP UP IN LIFE.

Starting Activity

Breathe, yes breathe, in to the count of 5, exhale counting to 5 slowly and repeat 7 times.

Why read this book and how will it help you?

Ok, let us continue, as I said, please replace worry/ anxiety with joy and happiness. **Happiness is a habit** and you have to train yourself to be happy.

So, if you are tired of feeling powerless, being overwhelmed, if your life is in limbo and you have low energy, if you feel strained, drained, used, abused, misused, heavily burdened, constantly having bad luck, or maybe being spiritually attacked, or if you feel emotionally weak or in severe debt, voiceless, invisible, shunned, ostracised. Or if you feel that you are being pushed over the edge.

Know that you are not alone! **This Self-Discovery toolkit, Journey Journal is for YOU!!!**

It is meant to help you be the **good, better, best** version of yourself, if you choose to act...NOW!... in this moment. I would love to work with you. I would like to work through your emotional trauma to help you to heal. However, you have to choose to be open-minded, release, and relax your heart, mind, body and spirit.

You need to decide to commit to becoming self-disciplined. To take full responsibility, full accounta-bility and full ownership of who you become from this point onwards.

Warning: this book will be fun, fair and firm. It will be highly focussed and solutions-oriented. However, it is up to you as to the extent and impact of your actual outcomes.

Note your feelings:

_____

_____

_____

_____

_____

_____

_____

_____

_____

_____

How to use this book

You are free to dip in into a chapter which relates to your current situation and resonates with you. Or, if you wish, read the whole book (highly recommended) by doing the following:

1. Read each specific chapter
2. Do the exercises in and at the end of every chapter with immediate implementation
3. Reflect on how the quotes make you feel and **please, please, please** do the relaxation exercises.

Understand, you have a new friend in me, so if you wish for help, I am here, I am here to help you find your gifts out of a crisis.

This is not simply a book, this is a gift to you, to build you up from the inside out and to help you maintain, sustain and achieve your dreams.

This self-discovery toolkit is both food and fuel for you to take action. It is here to help you create a new wavelength, frequency, or vibration of your thinking, which will enable you to take action and positively create a lifestyle that you desire.

This book is written from a place of love. Please understand, I am not perfect, nor do I profess to be so. However, what I do know is that there are people in this world that need help, and I believe that I can help you.

Listen, I have come out of a valley of darkness and I care enough to share with you the right to honour yourself, to respect yourself, to value yourself, to be kind, nurturing, forgiving, nourishing and encouraging to yourself.

You deserve so much more out of your life. This is a form of light energy to guide you, that you can take action NOW! After all, you are blessed and a blessing, and most importantly, totally unique. Yes, you have something to share to the world that will make a world of difference.

Benefits

It's about how to positively build yourself from a broken relationship from: family, friends, partner, colleagues, organisations and others.

This book has been written with you in mind. It is a self-help discovery guide, a toolkit equipped to move you from being crushed, scattered and invisible, to being visible, doing and having the life that you deserve.

Is this you? Final note

This self-discovery healing journey is specially designed with you in mind. Especially if you know what it feels like to be sick and tired, where there is more month than money. When enough is enough! I know that you deserve more out of your life and that you are looking for a way, to make a way, to the life that your desire and deserve.

I understand that you want to move out of your current situation and that you are now ready to take massive action to change your life. If this is true for you, great!!! This self-discovery healing journey journal is for you!

However, if at this point you are NOT ready, that is OK too. Why not do something really good and give this book to someone that you care about and who will actually use the tools inside this book to transform their life. Thank you.

Secret Page (Just for you xxx)

1. What are you holding in?

_____

_____

_____

_____

_____

_____

_____

2. What is/are your secret(s)

_____

_____

_____

_____

_____

_____

How to use this book

3. Are these secret(s) holding you prisoner?

   _____

4. Do you want to set yourself free and truly live?

   _____

Please Act

You are now ready to turn over a new page and
chapter of your life xxx

*Please email: Help@crushedtosparkle.com
and in the title section write:
I am working on my secrets!*

PLEASE, DO NOT TELL ME YOUR SECRETS,
*simply just send me a sentence on how you will feel
when you have worked/overcome/achieved
these secret matters.*

Crushed to Sparkle

Book Summary

The Model	Attention Focus	Outcomes, I am..
Break down	Alone	1. Wanting to move out of Isolation from the valley or dark place/space
Build up	Awake	1. "Awakening out of what seemed a hopeless situation"
Breakthrough	Aspiring	1. Transitioning as the phoenix rises from the ashes, rising out of the black hole.
Break Free	Alignment	1. Transforming into a BRAND-NEW YOU, 2. Loving yourself in a non-egotistical way. 3. Moving forward in your life. 4. Able to maintain and sustain your happiness

Chapter 1

Breakdown

"Who are you to judge the life I live? I know I'm not perfect—and I don't live to be—but before you start pointing fingers, make sure your hands are clean!"

Bob Marley

"Impossible is just a big word thrown around about by small men who find it easier to live in the world they've been given than to explore the power they have been given to change it"

Muhammad Ali

"What is your approach and how to overcome criticism?"

Let us talk—Raw and Rock Bottom!!!

Ok, in order to do better, you need to look at yourself and decide that you are now willing to positively take action to make a change in your life. That you are willing to be a student and learn to master your life.

In this chapter, we learn to declutter your mind. After all, a messy environment reflects a messy mind and life!

So, are you ready to take the first step?

_____

I warn you — it will be painful. However, what would you prefer — live out the rest of your life the way you are living now?

_____

Or do you really want to change?

_____

I'll be blunt. If you do not take control of your life, then you, by default, are letting others run and control, dictate and rearrange your life. You simply become a puppet, with others pulling your strings. Is that really what you want out of your life?

_____

I am asking you honestly — will you continue to be a spectator in your life and not an active player? Listen and listen well, know that you are worthy, wonderful, amazing, abundant, beautiful, creative, talented, knowledgeable, outstanding. Yes, YOU, I am talking to you! Do not look away, yes, you may laugh as you may not currently see yourself in that way; however, that is alright, you are, after all, a work in progress!

Maybe you are feeling sore, painful inside, afraid, alone, vulnerable, distrustful, exposed and so on and so forth?

_____

I ask, when you look in the mirror, do you criticise yourself, or do you affirm yourself?

_____

Does your mood change erratically, i.e. one minute you are feeling happy and then in an instant, someone says something to you and you become absolutely LIVID!!!

Do you turn to someone or something to make you feel better?

_____

What / who is it that you turn to?

_____

_____

_____

Does this thing have complete hold over you, e.g. drinking, smoking, chocolate, cakes, biscuits, promiscuity?

_____

Are you taking full responsibility for your life and actions, or are you blaming the world for your current situation?

_____

Let me ask you, are you really ready and willing to ask for and implement the help offered?

_____

Yes, I hear you say. Great, so let us now look at some mind shifting questions, shall we?

_____

Chapter 1 Activities

Activity 1: Authentic YOU

1. Before we begin, please write down what is the lowest point, event, situation in your life right now. For example, what is stopping, hurting, harming you?

_____

_____

_____

2. What is your biggest threat?

_____

_____

_____

3. Also take a selfie/photo of you right now! Yes, a photograph! Why? Because by the end of this journey journal you can look back at who you WERE and see that it is not who you are NOW!

4. Did you take the selfie?

_____

If **YES** great this is your first step to making a positive change in your life.

5. If **NO**, Why?

_____

_____

_____

OK, now take the picture and also answer the question about your lowest point below. Look, I am holding your hand, we will work through this. Please trust in the process and know that you are not alone. OK, now **PLEASE do Activity 1**. Yes, smile, I am smiling, right back at you xxx

Please be honest, I am here to help you to help yourself. Understand that you are not alone. Do not be downcast; we will find a way for you to move out of what you perceive as impossible.

Ok, smile, come on, smile with me, we can get through this as we are a T.E.A.M (Together, Everyone, Achieves More)

Activity 2: Facing your Fears

Here are some mind-jogging questions:

1. Who or what is stopping you?

_____

_____

_____

_____

2. Why is this thing or person stopping you?

_____

_____

_____

_____

3. When did this all begin?

_____

_____

_____

Be as descriptive as you need to, as the more you release the knots of your life the more you will be able to create balance in your mind, body and spirit.

4. How are you honestly feeling about this current situation?

_____

_____

_____

_____

_____

5. What do you really want out of **YOUR** life?

_____

_____

_____

_____

6. Which way will you go from here? E.g. forwards, backwards, sideways, diagonally?

_____

Activity 3: Mirror Work:
Body Confidence challenge

Go to a full-length mirror and undress yourself in front of the mirror.

1. As you stand naked, how do you feel? For example: Do you feel great?

_____

_____

_____

_____

2. What do you notice? For example, body challenges, over or underweight?

_____

_____

_____

_____

3. Why do you feel like this?

I feel like this Because _____

_____

_____

4. What would you like to see differently?

_____

_____

5. If this were to change, whose benefit would it be for? Is it for you or others?

_____

_____

_____

6. Now, supposing you are unable to change that thing, then what?

_____

_____

_____

Activity 4: Food, glorious food

Now let me ask you a few questions:

1. Do you see food as your medicine?

   _____

2. What does your food cupboards, fridge, freezer contents say about you?

   _____

   _____

   _____

   _____

3. Water intake—How many glasses of water do you drink per day?

   _____

4. Write a food diary for the next 7 days. See if there is a pattern as to what, when, why, how you are eating your food. E.g. eating in a rush, standing when eating, eating on the go, or not eating?

Food Diary Table

Day	Breakfast	Lunch	Supper	Snacks
Monday				
Tuesday				
Wednesday				
Thursday				
Friday				
Saturday				
Sunday				

Activity 5: Sleep Patterns

1. What time do you go to sleep?

   _____

2. How long do you sleep?

   _____

3. How would you describe the quality of your sleep?

   _____

4. What do you think needs to be improved?

   _____

Activity 6: Physical Exercises

1. Do you exercise? Yes/No,

   _____

   If Yes….

2. What time do you exercise?

   _____

3. How long do you exercise?

_____

4. Where do you exercise?

_____

_____

5. How many days of the week do you exercise?

_____

6. How do you feel after you have exercised?

_____

_____

_____

Activity 7: See and treat yourself as royalty, as we all go through some rough stuff!

Do better, be better, have betterment. What will you treat yourself today and this week, if you achieve positive steps towards your goal?

Fill your answer in the table on the next page.

Breakdown

Goal Treat Table

Day	Goal	Treat	Accomplishment
Monday			
Tuesday			
Wednesday			
Thursday			
Friday			
Saturday			
Sunday			

Activity 8: What would be your ideal reality?

Write down below what that looks like and enjoy taking ownership of your life!

_____

_____

_____

_____

_____

_____

_____

_____

_____

_____

_____

Emotional Freedom Breakdown Analysis

Behaviour	Cause of Behaviour	Attachment To	Result
Validation from others to work harder	No self-love...no inner compass	Approval to work harder	The stakes will move upward each time
Comparing self with others	No love for self . . . attachment and insecurity	Need to have others for comparison with self . . . dependency	Dependency grows as I move away from self
Success of others makes me feel inadequate	No love for self.... insecurity and jealously	Others' failure to make me feel good	The feeling of inadequacy grows as I see success in others
Needing praise for good deeds	No love for self . . . emptiness, dissatisfaction	Praise from others for good deeds	Will get less praise for 'good' deeds
Loving others to get approval	No self knowledge . . . . confused, doubtful, suspicious, apprehensive	Being lobbied by others	Love is conditional . . . constant approval is impossible

Crushed to Sparkle

"If you have no confidence in self, you are twice defeated in the race of life"

Marcus Garvey

"Defeat is a state of mind; No one is ever defeated until defeat has been accepted as a reality"

Bruce Lee

"To spend time is to pass it in a specified manner. To waste time is to expend it thoughtlessly or carelessly. We all have time to either spend or waste and it is our decision what to do with it. But once passed, it is gone forever."

Bruce Lee

Chapter 2

Build Up

"Yesterday is gone. Tomorrow has not yet come. We have only today. Let us begin."

> *Mother Teresa*

"You are what you think"

> *Confucius*

"Every new beginning comes from some other beginning's end."

> *Seneca*

"Be the kind of person that you want people to think you are."

> *Socrates*

"It does not matter how slowly you go so long as you do not stop".

> *Confucius*

"Kind words can be short and easy to speak, but their echoes are truly endless."

Mother Teresa

"I am not teaching you anything. I just help you to explore yourself"

Bruce Lee

"To move the world, we must move ourselves"

Socrates

"Be faithful in small things because it is in them that your strength lies".

Mother Teresa

"I am awake, I am aware, what are my choices?"

Wakey, Wakey, now that you are awake, let us build you up, shall we? Are you ready?

_____

YES, I hear you, say great job! Then let us skip the next few paragraphs and go to the **over to you tasks** below!

Build Up

If NO!

What has happened today?

_____

_____

_____

_____

Has something upset you?

_____

Are you letting someone else's opinion become your reality?

_____

Ummm, if so, <u>please repeat the first chapter!</u> I am here to coach you, but only as long as you wish to be coached. I am here to support you…if you wish to be supported. I am here to listen to your cries and wipe your tears, if you really want the help. However, first and foremost, you have to be present to your feelings, right here and right now **and take personal responsibility for your actions and your life!**

Wow, yes, that may sound harsh, but unless you choose to make a change, then your life will simply stay the same, so what is it going to be...... I will wait for you.

Ask yourself how long will you keep on making excuses?

_____

Ask yourself how long will you keep finding distractions in order **NOT** to get focused and organised?

_____

OK, please take a moment and breathe, we need to relax. Come on now, let us breathe, OK, Juliyah, I am alive, therefore, I AM breathing!!!

Yes, that is true; however, I would like you to open your mind and consider "deep stomach breathing". This will help you heal you from the inside out.

Are you now ready to proceed?

_____

Is that Yes, I hear… great!

So Juliyah, how do I do deep belly breathing? …

You complete the next activity that is how.

Chapter 2 Activities

Activity 1: Deep belly breathing

Instructions for the Breathing activity:

1. Simply find a quiet space

2. Sit down

3. Close your eyes

4. Place your palms flat on your lower abdomen, just below your belly button

5. Then inhale through your nose for a count of 6 or more (whatever you are comfortable with)

6. Fill your lower stomach below the belly button,

7. Then, hold your breath for half of the time on step 5 (inhalation time, e.g. if you breathed in for 6 seconds then hold for 3 seconds.

8. Then exhale slowly, with purpose and intent through your mouth bringing in your lower stomach towards your back (imagine a deflated balloon).

Repeat this process 7 times.

How are you feeling now? Good! Great!

Now let us get to the 'over to you' tasks, OK?

Activity 2: 'Over to YOU' tasks

1. Start the day with an attitude of gratitude — when you open your eyes, give thanks for life to see another day. Say a prayer if you will.

2. Create gratitude statements **(I am so happy and grateful now, that..........)**

3. Purchase and use a notebook as a <u>Build-up journal</u> for yourself; this will be your own invaluable tool to becoming the good, better, best version of yourself.

4. Next take action to live, create, innovate and transform your life; do something different today.

5. Be aware of your breathing, create relaxing moments throughout the day.

6. Check your posture, stance, tonality and your presence (what energy are you bringing to places and people you meet each day?)

Build Up

Have a vision and then take steps to create some goals to achieve the vision.

You may wonder, 'how do I do that?'

I have clarity in my vision and goals by answering these questions.

a. Identify what is it that you really want?

_____

_____

_____

_____

_____

b. Know what is urgent in your life.

_____

_____

_____

_____

_____

c. Who are your diamonds (precious people in your life)?

_____

_____

_____

_____

_____

d. Why do you want these things? Create a strong heart-felt emotional WHY, and really understand WHY this is important to you.

_____

_____

_____

_____

_____

e. In what time frame do you want to achieve your goal, e.g. 1 month, 3 months etc.

_____

Build Up

f. How can you break this goal into bite-size chunks?

_____

_____

_____

_____

_____

_____

_____

_____

_____

_____

_____

_____

_____

g. You should aim to break these goals into monthly, weekly, daily, hourly tasks.

Goal Table

Monthly Goals	Daily Goals	Hourly Goals

Build Up

h. Also add how your goals will aspire and inspire you daily life.

_____

_____

_____

i. Create a state of expectancy (I will do x by y date!)

I will _____

_____

By _____

I will _____

_____

By _____

I will _____

_____

By _____

Crushed to Sparkle

I will _____

_____

By _____

I will _____

_____

By _____

I will _____

_____

By _____

I will _____

_____

By _____

I will _____

_____

By _____

Build Up

j. What is it going to take, to motivate you into action?

_____

k. What emotions would you need to feel in order to regain motivation?

_____

l. What emotion do you feel now that is making you lack motivation? For example: Fear

_____

m. Why is it that this emotion causes you to lack motivation? For example: rejection/ridicule

_____

n. When you do not feel like doing something? For example: all the time, sometimes, etc.

_____

_____

_____

_____

o. Question yourself as to what is really urgent in your life.

_____

_____

_____

_____

_____

p. What is it going to take to take action?

_____

_____

_____

_____

_____

q. Do you want more or do you want less pain?

_____

Build Up

r. What are you holding onto and why?

    For Example: pain, hurt, loss, replay, past event

    _____

    _____

    _____

    _____

s. So... do you **REALLY** want to confront your fears
    and defeat these blockages; move out of being stuck
    and having doubtful moments

                        _____

t. What do you love doing and why?

    _____

    _____

    _____

    _____

    _____

u. Let go, do not hold on any longer to these negative limiting beliefs. Let the universe work in your life. Will you do that?

_____

v. Please, please, please, learn to give and take and not simply just take from others, be ethical, be honest and have integrity!

w. Ask yourself How can you help others as well. Example: I Can…

I Can _____

_____

I Can _____

_____

I Can _____

_____

I Can _____

_____

Build Up

I Can _____

_____

I Can _____

_____

I Can _____

_____

I Can _____

_____

I Can _____

_____

I Can _____

_____

"There is no better than adversity. Every defeat, every heartbreak, every loss, contains its own seed, its own lesson on how to improve your performance next time."

Malcolm X

"If I cannot do great things, I can do small things in a great way."

Martin Luther King

"Your life is what your thoughts make it."

Confucius

"If you can't fly then run, if you can't run then walk, if you can't walk then crawl, but whatever you do you have to keep moving forward."

Martin Luther King

"Get up Stand up, Stand up for your rights. Get up Stand up, don't give up the fight."

Bob Marley

"We must accept finite disappointment, but never lose infinite hope."

Martin Luther King

"Only a man who knows what it is like to be defeated can reach down to the bottom of his soul and come up with the extra ounce of power it takes to win when the match is even."

Muhammad Ali

Chapter 3

Breakthrough

"The best way to make your dreams come true is to wake up"

Muhammad Ali

"Always try to associate with people from whom you can learn something. All the knowledge that you want is in the world, and all you have to do is go and seek it."

Marcus Garvey

"None but ourselves can free our mind"

Bob Marley

"The mind alone is one's friend as well as one's enemy."

Bhagavad Gita

"Good actions give strength to ourselves and inspire good actions in others."

Plato

"Men who are in earnest are not afraid of consequences Breakthrough."

Marcus Garvey

"If you spend too much time thinking about a thing, you'll never get it done. Make at least one definite move daily toward your goal."

Bruce Lee

"The ultimate measure of a man is not where he stands in moments of comfort and convenience, but where he stands at times of challenge and controversy."

Martin Luther King

"The possession of anything begins in the mind."

Bruce Lee

"Open our eyes, look within. Are you satisfied with the life you're living?"

Bob Marley

Take action to adapt and create

Congratulations, you are right on track for transitioning to your big breakthrough. This is your path to freedom and satisfaction.

Build Up

In this chapter, you will learn to stand for something. You will know that this is your time. You are ready to make meaningful collaborative relationships and effective ethical networking too! Looking back in chapter 1 we went over all the issues that you have with yourself, as well as how others perceived you. In chapter 2 we have gone over what you want you to become and how you would like yourself and others to perceive you.

Here we will be working on implementing simple steps that you need to take in order to reach the goals that you have set in chapter 2.

Making changes is not easy but with the activities repeated on a regular basis you will be able to assess your progress and find the areas that you need to improve on to reach your goals.

If you need more support in getting to the right mindset please email for assistance at Help@crushedtosparkle.com

If you are ready…

Great!!!!

For the next steps we can get started with the take action activities that will clarify a few simple steps to improve your personal view of yourself and to help you achieve your goals.

Chapter 3 Activities

Activity 1: Adaptation and Action Steps

1. Be happy NOW!
2. See the best in others, yes, I know this can and will be difficult; however, just keep on keeping on.
3. Be the best version of yourself!
4. Understand that you are a gemstone.
5. Know that you have an illuminating loving, caring and sharing heart.
6. Step up and show up in life by revealing your brilliance, especially your **goldmine mind!!!**
7. Have an attitude of gratitude and look forward to your journey of "becoming" into the good, better, best version of you.
8. Face your fears
9. Pick up the key and unlock your potential
10. Surround yourself with people with the same vibrational frequency as yourself, ie similar or better outlook on life!
11. Know that you have the power to release
12. If life was a game, then fulfil your expectancy
13. Be anchored and grounded
14. Know that your best is good enough
15. Now go ahead and create the life that you desire

Have you worked on the above steps?

_____

Build Up

If NO, why?

_____

_____

_____

_____

_____

If YES, great!!

How has your life changed so far?

_____

_____

_____

_____

_____

_____

_____

How do you see yourself in the mirror now, compared to how you saw yourself back in chapter 1?

_____

_____

_____

_____

How does your new life make you feel?

_____

_____

_____

_____

What challenges are you still facing with the new changes?

_____

_____

_____

_____

Build Up

We are now in 2020, and this year is your year!

To be honest, **this book is timeless!**

**However, whatever year you are blessed
to receive this book, then that moment,
that year, Is your year to conquer!**

To be a Champion, an enlightened warrior, king or queen. Know that you are phenomenal, you are amazing, so RISE UP and shine brightly. After all, you are a DIAMOND, so sparkle!

Can I share something with you?

You have brilliance in you!

*Your mind is a goldmine, so dig deep and recover
and rediscover who you are!*

*YES, you are filled with spiritual energy, living in a
body, seeking experiences!*

So what other experiences will you give to yourself?

_____

_____

_____

Did you know that:

1. There is a micro universe within you that matches the macro universe? Please know that you can unfold by adapting and adjusting to moments in time without losing your essence.

2. The one fastest to take action gets the job done! So, stop procrastinating and use your time wisely. Keep pushing forward, keep going, get focused!

3. **YOU are a multi-dimensional person,**

   a. You have the power to create your future you NOW!

   b. Look out for glimpses of intuition when you are still and allow the universe to speak into your being.

4. You should constantly observe:

   a. Your company

   b. Your heart

   c. Your body

   d. Your mind

   e. Your quiet time!

Build Up

Activity 2: Don't give up, don't quit. Your time is NOW

1. Yes, you have got a challenge, so what!

2. What are you going to do about it?

_____

_____

_____

_____

3. How will you be able to overcome it?

_____

_____

_____

_____

4. Well, just keep moving, keep going, do not give up, you have to be your own cheerleader!!!

   a. Have you become your own cheerleader?

   _____

If **YES** Great… If **NO**, Why?

_____

_____

5. You have to pat yourself on the back.

   a. Did you do that?

                                      _____

If **YES** Great… If **NO**, Why?

_____

_____

6. You have to tell yourself how great you are!

   a. Did you do that?

                                        _____

If **YES** Great… If **NO**, Why?

_____

_____

7. You have to create the life that you deserve. Only you can create that life and value that life.

    a. Did you believe this?

    _____

    If **YES** Great… If **NO**, Why?

    _____

    _____

8. You have to declutter you mind, body, spirit and environment, in the home, car, and work!

    a. Will you do this?

    _____

    If **YES** when?

    _____

    If **NO**, Why?

    _____

    _____

    d. Will you improve your networks to determine and improve your net worth?

_____

If **YES** when?

_____

If **NO**, Why?

_____

_____

By following a few simple and personal rules you can ensure your personal growth and development and your ability to embrace the bliss of living in the **power of now**!

A few of the rules that I have found to be most effective come down to a total of **15 critical points**.

I suggest that you keep a copy of these rules by your bedside or on the fridge so that you can see them daily and remind yourself of what you need to do.

Build Up

Good Rules to go by

1. Be happy NOW
2. Love imperfection
3. Bless and send those who put you down thoughts of love as love softens
4. Be still
5. Be grateful, thankful and passionate in your purpose, vision, goals.
6. Be self-determined, live on purpose, in passion, with faith, and most importantly, take steps to make yourself proud!
7. Minimize complaining, adopt a habit of gratitude and **take action, take action, take action.**
8. Look to do good in any given situation as much as you can
9. See the positive out of a negative
10. Feed and feel your goals daily
11. Look to see the best in others. Be an encourager, empower others to do the same.
12. You are a gift of this moment
13. Realise now that you are transitioning to transform
14. Know that life will present you with many challenges. However, you have the power within to overcome, so dig deep my friend and you will uncover your **DIAMONDS** that will change your life. Dig deep my friend and you will strike **GOLD**!!!
15. Know that you both give and receive energy in every aspect of your being.

"Be kind, for everyone you meet is fighting a hard battle."

Plato

"If you always put limit on everything you do, physical or anything else. It will spread into your work and into your life. There are no limits. There are only plateaus, and you must not stay there, you must go beyond them."

Bruce Lee

"We cannot live better than in seeking to become better."

Socrates

"When it is obvious that the goals cannot be reached, do not adjust the goals, adjust the action steps."

Confucius

"It is not a daily increase, but a daily decrease. Hack away at the inessentials."

Bruce Lee

Build Up

"The time is always right to do what is right."
Martin Luther King

"Just because you are happy it does not mean that the day is perfect but that you have looked beyond its imperfections."
Bob Marley

"Adapt what is useful, reject what is useless, and add what is specifically your own."
Bruce Lee

"There is no harm in repeating a good thing."
Plato

Reflective Notes:

_____

_____

_____

_____

_____

_____

_____

_____

_____

_____

_____

_____

Chapter 4

Break Free

"Our greatest glory is not in never falling, but in rising every time we fall."

Confucius

"If you have no confidence in self, you are twice defeated in the race of life."

Marcus Garvey

"Ambition is the desire to go forward and improve one's condition. It is a burning flame that lights up the life of the individual and makes him see himself in another state. To be ambitious is to be great in mind and soul. To want that which is worthwhile and strive for it. To go on without looking back, reaching to that which gives satisfaction."

Marcus Garvey

"Little by little, through patience and repeated effort, the mind will become stilled in the Self."

Bhagavad Gita

"An unexamined life is not worth living."

Socrates

"Let him that would move the world, first move himself."

Socrates

"The mind alone is one's friend as well as one's enemy."

Bhagavad Gita

Break free—Transformation - New YOU!!! A BRAND CALLED YOU!!!!

You are now in the **stretch zone**; you have moved out of your comfort zone. You have taken risks, overcome challenges and now you are feeling good and looking great. However, you are not complacent and you know that there will always be challenges in life. The difference now is that you possess the tools to overcome these challenges as you have built yourself from the inside out!

Break Free

Right now, you are outrageously creative, innovative, and you are working and performing at an unstoppable, indomitable spirit level. You now have an abundance mentality; you are not surviving — you are living...you are living the life that you truly desire and deserve.

Aaaaahhhh, Juliyah, I am not fully there yet! Please help! Certainly, I do get carried away with the passion that I see inside you. I have enjoyed our journey together, through your life so far, so please forgive me for really celebrating your future you, right here, right now!

OK, in this phase and stage of this self-discovery journey, you will find your gifts, your passion and your purpose!

OK, I hear, so let us begin with the power of NOW. This is the time to purposefully take full responsibility, full ownership and to be fully accountable to someone for the actions that you will take from here on in!

Chapter 4 Activities

Activity 1: Abundance mentality

Abundance mentality, what does that mean to you?

_____

_____

_____

_____

_____

_____

_____

_____

_____

_____

_____

Activity 2: Finding out your gifts out of your crisis

1. What do you like (doing) and why?

_____

_____

_____

_____

_____

2. What do you watch and why?

_____

_____

_____

_____

_____

3. What do you listen to and why?

_____

_____

_____

_____

_____

_____

4. Who do you admire and why?

_____

_____

_____

_____

_____

_____

5. What do others say about you time and time again? (we are working only with positive constructive feedback!)

_____

_____

_____

_____

_____

_____

6. What clues are hidden in your childhood and teenage years?

_____

_____

_____

_____

_____

_____

7. What were your dreams as a child?

_____

_____

_____

_____

_____

_____

Now review what you have written

Identify what job or job creation is now possible based on who you are and what you like to do.

8. Write down your job, or new job creation here

_____

_____

_____

_____

9. So now, do you want to work for someone else, if yes, why?

_____

_____

_____

_____

10. Do you want to work full or part time?

_____

11. Do you now want to work for yourself, if yes, why?

_____

_____

_____

_____

_____

_____

_____

Keep up the great work

Listen my king or queen, you are doing a really great job right about now! Congratulations! Now, have you also considered working full-time, part time as well as working part time on your business to see which one feels right for you?

Activity 3: I am........

Next, you need to create your own mantra below, for example:

"I am ...... creative, beautiful, powerful, enlightened, prayerful, warrior, queen/king"

I am _____

_____

I am _____

_____

I am _____

_____

I am _____

_____

Activity 4: Streamline your life. How?

1. Remove the distractions and energy suckers/drainers (people/things)

2. Remove objects and people who are not serving your best interests. In other words, de-clutter to free the flow of energy in your space.

3. Be forensic around your house; go through room by room, as every bit of space needs to be examined and cleared or streamlined.

4. Repeat this de-clutter process for your:

   a. Work environment:

   b. Friends

   c. Family

   d. Work colleagues

   e. Identify essential courses (Implementing courses)

Did you streamline your life?

_____

If **NO**, Why?

_____

_____

If **YES** Great…

Now, can you not feel that you are a Phoenix risen from the ashes? You are on fire and you are walking in and on fire. You have now found your purpose and your passion, so now become a leader! Become a leader in your industry!!! Believe, Achieve, Succeed!!!

Activity 5: Your NEW work

1. What is your field of work now and how do you feel about the change?

   _____

   _____

   _____

   _____

2. How will you make a difference in your work?

   _____

   _____

   _____

   _____

3. How will you add value and improve the customer experience, or journey? (Client Relationship Management)

_____

_____

_____

Break free to transformation after all.
You are now a brand.
Called New Me,
Unique Me,
Original Me.

Activity 6: Living Legacy

1. What does Living Legacy look like for you?

_____

_____

_____

_____

Activity 7: Community Unity

1. Now are you ready to work towards Community Unity, what does it look like for you?

_____

_____

_____

_____

_____

_____

_____

_____

_____

_____

_____

Activity 8: Review your dreams

1. Now review your dreams for the next year 3 years, 5 years, 7 years, 9 years, 11 years, 15 years, 20 years or 25 years.

    Dare to dream very big.

Dream Timeline	Dream									
Years	1 Year	3 Years	5 Years	7 Years	9 Years	11 Years	15 Years	20 Years	25 Years	

"Know, that you know, that you know, that you now step and operate from a divine connection with infinite source energy"

Juliyah Brown

2. Now respect & demand more from yourself (please complete)

I must _____

_____

Because I can _____

_____

I must do _____

_____

Because I can _____

_____

Activity 9: Smile

Now **SMILE, on purpose!** go that extra mile, please smile as you say: "I love me." Smile on your inside, do appreciate your amazing mind, body and soul, and all that goodness will be reflected and outpoured on the outside!!!

Remember

"I am a brand called ME!"

"I am an author, artist, architect of my life.".

Now you are soaring—

1. So write down your next steps by harnessing your insights from your personal and professional development so far.

_____

_____

_____

_____

Activity 10: Your history, your poetry in motion, your love note!!

Write your own poem or story, a personal love note to yourself, of your progress through the four chapters.

_____

_____

_____

_____

_____

_____

_____

_____

_____

_____

_____

_____

Activity 11: PARTY TIME

I invite you to:

A. Read the lyrics to these songs.

B. Then watch and listen to the videos.

C. Next, write down if any of the songs resonated with you.

D. Finally, see if any of these songs provided you with any further insights and more clarity into your life.

1. 702: Where my girls at
2. Aaliyah: One in a million
3. Aaliyah: Try again
4. Aaliyah: We need a resolution
5. Amerie: One thing
6. Angie Stone, featuring Alicia Keys and Eve: Brotha part II
7. Angie Stone: Brotha
8. Aretha Franklin: Respect
9. Ashanti: Always on time
10. Ashanti: Foolish
11. Ashanti: Rain on me
12. Ashanti: Rock with me
13. Bell Bev Devoe: Poison
14. Beyoncé: Best thing I never had
15. Beyoncé: Listen
16. Beyoncé: My halo
17. Blackstreet: Before I let you go

18. Blackstreet: Joy
19. Bob Marley: Get up stand up
20. Bob Marley: Natural Mystic
21. Bobby Brown: My prerogative
22. Boyz II men: End of the Road
23. Boyz II men: Mother
24. Cherelle ft Alexander O'Neal: Saturday love
25. Cheryl Lynn: Got to be real
26. Christina Aguilera: Beautiful
27. Ciara: One two step
28. D'Angelo: Brown Sugar
29. Destiny child: So good, so good
30. Destiny's Child: Girl
31. Destiny's Child: Independent Woman's
32. Destiny's Child: Survivor
33. Digable Planets: Rebirth of the Slick
34. Earth Wind and Fire: Enough is Enough
35. Earth Wind and Fire: Groove to night
36. Earth Wind and Fire: September
37. En Vogue: Don't let go
38. En Vogue: Free your mind
39. Erykah Badu: On and On
40. Faith Evans (Waiting to exhale)
41. Gwen Guthrie: Ain't nothing going on but the rent.
42. Herbie Hancock: Rockit
43. Jaheim: Put that woman First
44. Janet Jackson: That's the way love goes
45. Jennifer Lopez: My love does not cost a thing

46. Jill Scott: A Long Walk
47. Jill Scott: Golden
48. Joe: All the things
49. Karyn white: I'm not your Superwoman
50. Kirk Franklin: Looking Forward
51. Kool and the Gang: Celebrations
52. Lauryn Hill: Doo-wop (That thing)
53. Li Mo 4ever: Fabulous
54. LL Cool J: Knock you out
55. Luther Vandross: A House is not a Home
56. Luther Vandross: Dance with my Father
57. Luther Vandross: Endless
58. Luther Vandross: If only for 1 night
59. Luther Vandross: Love won't make me wait
60. Luther Vandross: Never to much
61. Luther Vandross: So Amazing
62. Luther Vandross: The Closer I get to you
63. M Beat Ft General Levy Junglist Massive
64. Mantronix: Got to have your love
65. Mario: How do I breathe
66. Marvin Gaye: Sexual healing
67. Mary J Blige: All that I can say
68. Mary J Blige: Be Happy (Official Matt X Version)
69. Mary J Blige: Be without you
70. Mary J Blige: Everything
71. Mary J Blige: Family Affair
72. Mary J Blige: I Am
73. Mary J Blige: I Love you

74. Mary J Blige: I try
75. Mary J Blige: I'm going down
76. Mary J Blige: Just Fine
77. Mary J Blige: Love no Limit
78. Mary J Blige: No more drama in my life
79. Mary J Blige: Not Gon Cry
80. Mary J Blige: Reminisce Mary Mary: Heaven
81. Mary J Blige: Take me as I am
82. Mary J Blige: We Rise (I See the Future)
83. Mary J Blige: You remind me
84. Mary J Blige: Your Child
85. Mary J Blige ft. Brook Lynn: Enough Cryin
86. Mary J Blige ft. George Benson: Seven Days
87. Mary J Blige ft. Lil Kim: I Can love you
88. Mary J Blige ft. Ludacris: Runaway love
89. Mary Mary: Shackles (Praise You)
90. Mase: Tell what you want
91. Maze: Joy and Pain
92. Michael Jackson: Earth Song
93. Michael Jackson: Remember the times
94. Michael Jackson: Don't stop to get enough
95. Michael Jackson: Liberian Girl
96. Michael Jackson: Man in the mirror
97. Michael Jackson: Off the Wall (All his tracks)
98. Michael Jackson: Remember the Time
99. Michael Jackson: Rockin Robin
100. Michael Jackson: You are not alone
101. Miles Davis: So What
102. Millie Small: My boy lollipop

103. Monica and Brandy: The boy is mine
104. Nas: I can
105. Nat King Cole: Unforgettable
106. Nicole Renee: Strawberry
107. Notorious BIG: Big Poppa
108. Oleta Adams: Get Here
109. Pharrell: Happy
110. Public Enemy: Can't Truss
111. Public Enemy: Don't believe the Hype
112. Public Enemy: Harder than you think
113. Public Enemy: Rebel without a pause
114. Rihanna: Diamonds
115. Rihanna: Take a bow
116. Rolls Royce: Love don't live here anymore
117. Rubin Studdard: I need an Angel
118. Shanks & Big Foot: Sweet like Chocolate
119. Stevie Wonder: Ribbon in the Sky
120. Temptations: My Girl
121. The Fugees: Ready or not
122. The sounds of blackness: I believe
123. The sounds of blackness: Optimistic
124. TLC: Don't go chasing waterfalls
125. TLC: So I creep
126. Toni Braxton: Breathe again
127. Toni Braxton: He wasn't man enough
128. Tupac: Changes
129. Usher: Bad Girl
130. Usher: Burn
131. Usher: Pop Ya Collar

132. Usher: You make me wanna
133. Whitney Houston and CeCe Winans:
     Count on Me
134. Whitney Houston: All the Man that I need
135. Whitney Houston: Greatest Love of All
136. Whitney Houston: I'm Every Woman
137. Whitney Houston: It's alright, but it's Okay
138. Yolanda Adams (Anita Baker): You bring me
     Joy
139. Yolanda Adams: Be Blessed
140. Yolanda Adams: Victory

E. What else can you add and bring to your party?

_____

_____

_____

_____

_____

_____

_____

Final notes from Juliyah

I invite you to practice these statements as good rules to live by

1. I am selfless;
2. I am a work in progress;
3. I am not a finished article as I learn more, I know less, so I keep on learning;
4. I encourage and empower others to help themselves and to help others to do the same, to be the best version of themselves.

Through a process of Refinement

1. I am fortified: Stronger
2. I am Intensified: Heated on fire
3. I am Magnified: Larger than life
4. I am destined for greatness
5. I can create a new value system.
6. I am a diamond
7. I am a precious gift to the world xxx

Now

1. Live, Laugh, Love, Life
2. Have fun
3. Play
4. Love the life you live
5. Live the life you love
6. Be happy

Activity 12: Over to you

1. Please write down what is the highest point, event, situation in your life right now?

_____

_____

_____

_____

2. What is your greatest achievement?

_____

_____

_____

_____

3. **Take a selfie/photo of you right now!** Yes, a photograph, Why? Because who you were on page 5 is not who you are NOW!

Break Free

Look, I am no longer holding your hand; we walk side by side confident in who we are!!! You have worked on yourself and still continue to work on yourself. You have trusted in the process I shared with you, and you know wholeheartedly that you are not alone.

Yes, smile, I am smiling right back at you xxx

Please do remember to...

I. Register for the next crushed to sparkle

    a. Retreat

    b. Seminar

    c. Webinar

    d. Online courses

II. Register your interest for, me to be professional guest speaker at your next event

III. To send me your testimonies

We offer support networks, one-to-one coaching, consulting, group workshops and group coaching sessions as well as on and offline resources, so feel confident and know that you are not alone!!!

Activity 13: Congratulations

1. After reading this book up to this point, please write down below how you look and feel. What are your intentions and new mindset for your new life?

_____

_____

_____

_____

_____

_____

_____

_____

_____

Congratulations!

You have now broken free, now you can be outrageously creative/innovative. You can do, you can be, you can have it too!

Now that you know what you really want, now that you know that you are unstoppable, RISE UP and constantly and never endingly improve your current performance.

My king, my queen, my friend, you have an ABUNDANCE mentality. If you want more, simply add more value to what you are doing. So others will buy your product or service, as you will be meeting their needs with great value.

I am offering you in the next few chapters, Bonus gifts, FAST TRACK insights and a special VIP surprise for you to enjoy!

"A people without the knowledge of their past history, origin and culture is like a tree without roots.

Marcus Garvey

"An unexamined life is not worth living."

Socrates

"Liberate the minds of men and ultimately you will liberate the bodies of men."

Marcus Garvey

"Our greatest glory is not in never falling, but in rising every time we fall."

Confucius

"Let him that would move the world, first move himself."

Socrates

"Ambition is the desire to go forward and improve one's condition. It is a burning flame that lights up the life of the individual and makes him see himself in another state.

To be ambitious is to be great in mind and soul. To want that which is worthwhile and strive for it. To go on without looking back, reaching to that which gives satisfaction."

Marcus Garvey

"Little by little, through patience and repeated effort, the mind will become stilled in the Self."

Bhagavad Gita

"I am learning to understand rather than immediately judge or to be judged. I cannot blindly follow the crowd and accept their approach. I will not allow myself to indulge in the usual manipulating game of role creation.

Fortunately for me, my self-knowledge has transcended that and I have come to understand that life is best to be lived and not to be conceptualized.

I am happy because I am growing daily and I'm honestly, not knowing where the limit lies. To be certain, every day there can be a revelation or a new discovery. I treasure the memory of the past misfortunes. It has added more to my bank of fortitude."

Bruce Lee

"You must be shapeless, formless, like water. When you pour water in a cup, it becomes the cup. When you pour water in a bottle, it becomes the bottle. When you pour water in a teapot, it becomes the teapot. Water can drip and it can crash. Become like water my friend."

Bruce Lee

Reflective Notes

_____

_____

_____

_____

_____

_____

_____

_____

_____

Chapter 5

FAST TRACK
to Self-Discovery:
"Being a Brand-New Me"

So, you may be asking yourself, what does a brand new me look like it?

At this point, I really want you to create that person that you really want to be as you have all the tools inside of you.

You know that you are AMAZING!

You know that you are PHENOMENAL!

Just create you, as you cannot be anyone else!

You are UNIQUE!

You are SPECIAL!

You have so much that the world is waiting to see.

Yes, you, I am talking to you!

Your future self is no longer in the future, you can step into your future self now!

Just do it and live the life that you truly desire and deserve.

Chapter 5 Activities -SELF ANALYSIS

Activity 1 Thoughts feelings and emotions— Question your:

1. Belief
2. Values
3. Perception
4. Attitude
5. Thoughts
6. Feelings
7. Emotions
8. Actions

What could you do differently?

_____

_____

_____

_____

Will you do things differently?

_____

Activity 2: Personal insights—
What is holding you back?

Speak up and Speak out, you have something to say! What is it? Work on how you manage your time by looking at points 1-4

1. Focus - What are you focusing on?

   _____

   _____

2. Distractions - What is distracting you and why?

   _____

   _____

   _____

3. What are you really busy doing?

   Select A or B to finish the sentence.

   Are you...

   a. Using time wisely?
   b. Wasting your time frivolously?

   _____

4. Overwhelmed - What is making you feel over-whelmed?

_____

_____

_____

   a. What will you do to improve your current state?

_____

_____

_____

_____

_____

_____

   b. I suggest that you revisit the previous chapters in this book to help fortify yourself xxx

Activity 3: What does my life look like, feel like, smell like, taste like, sound like?

Write down your thoughts, answers in great detail.

_____

_____

_____

_____

_____

_____

_____

_____

_____

_____

Activity 4 Learning from defeat, criticism, rejection

Answer the following questions honestly:

1. Does defeat cause you to stop trying?

    _____

2. Is temporary defeat the same as failure?

    _____

3. What have you learned from this setback?

    _____

    _____

4. Do you know how to transform the negative into a positive and turn it into success in your life?

    a. **If YES**, then I encourage you to go ahead and do it

    b. **If NO**, then may I suggest you revisit the previous chapters in this journey journal, to help guide you xxx

Activity 5: Self Discipline

1. Can you hold your tongue when you get angry?

   _____

2. Do you have a habit of speaking before you think?

   _____

3. Do you easily get angry?

   _____

4. Do your emotions overpower your reasoning?

   _____

   a. If YES, what action steps will you take to improve your current situation?

_____

_____

_____

_____

Activity 6: My current situation

An example:

Positive:	Solution	Negative
I am alive	Every day is precious	Lack confidence in my belief
I am a mother	I need to do the best for my son	I do not give myself enough time to celebrate and appreciate myself
I am employed	I need to create my own business	I procrastinate in malting my life more empowering
Mum is alive	Mum is in her own house	Mum is temporarily in a care home
A few good friends	Quality is more important than quantity	Lots of negative people
Brother	Supportive	He needs to support himself more too
Son	Ambitious	Easily distracted
Believe in creator/creation	Abundance	Please show me some signs, I am still waiting

For a more in-depth workshop register at:
workshops@crushedtosparkle.com
in the subject title add
SELF ANALYSIS WORKSHOPS

Chapter 6

FAST TRACK:
Food for Thought on Broken Relationships Case studies

FOOD FOR THOUGHT

Case study abstracts food for thought and what will you do? Over to you!

Women with trust issues:

These are women who have been celibate for several years and not dated. Why? Because they were mentally, financially, physically, emotionally neglected. Or maybe they were forced to make a choice between an unborn child or keeping their partner, or women suffering from a broken engagement with their ex-finance and are afraid of being hurt again. So, what are you going to do about it?

I suggest you register your interest at
workshops@crushedtosparkle.com
in the subject title add
WOMEN WITH TRUSTS ISSUES WORKSHOPS

Addiction

Ask yourself the following questions regarding addiction:

1. Are you addicted to substances, food, sex or other?

_____

_____

_____

2. How does it make you feel in that moment?

_____

_____

_____

3. Is it sustainable?

_____

_____

_____

Food for Thought on Broken Relationships

4. Is it really helping you to heal a part of you that you are either holding or suppressing?

_____

_____

_____

5. Or are you expressing a feeling that no longer serves your greater good?

_____

_____

_____

_____

6. If you had an opportunity to change your life and recover from your addiction, would you take it?

_____

_____

_____

_____

7. Supposing that you could face that addiction, face that fear, worry, anxiety, doubt, obsession, would you do it?

_____

_____

_____

_____

8. What if you could label the feeling and find out the associated impact it is having on your body?

   a. Would you want to?

   _____

9. Would you be open to thinking about and working towards recovering from your addiction and making a change in your way of life?

_____

_____

_____

_____

Food for Thought on Broken Relationships

10. Why don't you take a moment to visualise an event trigger for your addiction and then identify how you feel, whilst in that moment?

_____

_____

_____

_____

_____

_____

Ask yourself these three questions: 1 line response

1. Could you let this feeling go?

_____

2. Would you let this feeling go?

_____

3. When would you let this feeling go?

_____

And now check in again; how are you feeling?

_____

Now, take a breath, think about it and ask yourself these three questions again.

1. Could you let this feeling go?

_____

2. Would you let this feeling go?

_____

3. When would you let this feeling go?

_____

Did you notice any difference after taking a breath?

_____

What was the difference?

_____

_____

Food for Thought on Broken Relationships

What if I told you that you could change you feeling in this moment?

1. Would you want to?

    _____

2. What do you feel like now?

    _____

3. How do you want to feel?

    _____

4. Are you willing to do what it takes to overcome the feeling you have now?

    _____

5. Are you willing to put in the work to overcome your addiction?

    _____

This is a self-help DIY process.

It is about releasing, letting go, letting things out and not keeping things in!

Do you understand!?

So, if you really want to make a change, you can, but it is entirely up to you!

So If you require a helping hand, then would you kindly register your interest at workshops@crushedtosparkle.com in the subject title add

ADDICTION WORKSHOPS

Overwhelmed in debt

If this is you, are you living off your overdraft facility, credit cards or loans?

_____

Are you constantly swapping between accounts, your pennies instead of pounds?

_____

Have you asked family and friends for help and shared with them your life story and AFTER telling them how extremely vulnerable you are, they simply said, "Oh sorry, I can't help you!"

So, what are you going to do right now to get out of debt?

_____

_____

Register your interest at
workshops@crushedtosparkle.com
in the subject title add
OVERWHELMED IN DEBT WORKSHOPS

Loss of a child

Are you a parent (mother) who has had a miscarriage or an abortion?

_____

Maybe because you had to make a choice of keeping the man and getting married and having no further children, or keeping the child and be a single parent and another statistic joining the single parent register and having the stigma of having another child with a different man.

If this is you, what have you done to help and aid your healing in order for you to forgive yourself for the hard sacrificial choices?

_____

_____

_____

_____

*Consider getting help by registering
your interest at:
workshops@crushedtosparkle.com
in the subject title add
LOSS OF A CHILD WORKSHOPS*

Food for Thought on Broken Relationships

Your relationship with your child / children

Are you trying to live out your dreams through your child / children?

_____

Are you making them do the things you did not do?

_____

Or are you asking or even demanding from them to do things that you did not get to do in your childhood?

_____

In essence, are you looking for a second chance to live out your childhood dreams through your children?

_____

Are you dictating their life, without allowing them to express their points of view, opinions or input into their own lives?

_____

Are there major differences of expectations in your household as a result of imposing your childhood dreams on your child / children?

_____

Are you facing constant clashes with your child / children?

_____

Does your child revert to wasting time, through social media, games, music, videos or arranging meeting up with friends, instead of them focusing on their studies, or helping around the house, or seriously thinking about what they want out of life or improving their grades etc?

_____

If this sums up your challenge, what are you actively doing about it?

_____

_____

_____

_____

Consider registering your interest at
workshops@crushedtosparkle.com
in the subject title add
MY RELATIONSHIP WITH
MY CHILD WORKSHOPS

Are you a CARER?

Are you a carer looking after a loved one? And is all the responsibility on your shoulders?

_____

Are the rest of the family members burying their heads in the sand or relentlessly criticising and scrutinising everything you do, yet, they never come up with solutions?

_____

Please answer the following questions

1. Are you a carer with no family at all?

   _____

2. Are you a young person who is the main carer for a family relative, namely your parents?

   _____

3. Have you had to put your dreams on hold?

   _____

4. Do you feel guilty that you actually want to do something for yourself and that you actually want a life, too?

   _____

5. As a carer, have your felt invisible or voiceless?

   _____

6. Have you been ostracized, or even bullied by family members?

   _____

7. Or people in your school, college, university, work or even siblings?

   _____

8. Have your requests for help been ignored by social services, Power of Attorney, organisations, courts, or other legal entities?

   _____

If you can relate to any or all of the above as a carer, what are you going to do to make a change?

How are you taking care of your own health and wellbeing/welfare?

Consider getting help and support through registering at: workshops@crushedtosparkle.com in the subject title add
CARERS WORKSHOPS

Single Parenting and the Education System

1. Does your child believe what the teachers say is correct?

    _____

2. Is your child acting in line with the establishments: **"Self-fulfilling Prophecy?"** As a parent, do you have a much higher standards and expectations of your child?

    _____

3. Are your challenging the schools to improve your child's grades and are you constantly asking them to not simply see and label your child as **"average"**. Do you ask for more support?

    _____

4. If so, do you follow up, if you do not get a response?

    _____

5. Do you attend parents' meetings?

    _____

6. Do you check what your child has been doing in school in great detail, or do you accept the vague response of, "We've done a lot of work today."

    _____

7. Have you ever asked yourself, what does that actually mean or involve?

_____

8. What activities outside of school do you do with your child to forge a stronger bond and create happy memories?

_____

9. Do you often hear the cliché line, "your child has potential"?

_____

10. Have you actually challenged the school as to HOW this potential will be realised?

_____

11. Are you a parent sick and tired of your child believing that they will always be an average student?

_____

If so, are you doing anything to change the way you deal with your child / children's education!

Food for Thought on Broken Relationships

12. What will you be doing to better support your child / children?

_____

_____

_____

_____

Consider getting help and support through
registering at: workshops@crushedtosparkle.com
in the subject title add:
SINGLE PARENTING AND THE EDUCATION
SYSTEM WORKSHOPS

Putting your dreams on hold

Are you putting your own dreams on hold in order to meet and support the dreams of others?

_____

Are you a carer who has to look after your children and your ageing-parents whilst other family members simply swan around and move ahead in their lives, and as they travel around the world whilst you are taking care of your parent, or loved ones.

_____

How does that make you feel?

_____

_____

_____

Is the cared for more interested in those children that are neglecting them, as opposed to the one showing some thought of consideration to the cared for, who is actually looking after them?

_____

Food for Thought on Broken Relationships

How does that make you feel?

_____

_____

Are you the carer who reduced your working hours to be able to find quality time to look after your loved ones?

_____

How does that make you feel?

_____

_____

Have you been close to or became homeless as you could not keep up with the rent or mortgage payments?

_____

How does that make you feel?

_____

_____

_____

If that's you, what are your doing to improve your current situation?

_____

_____

_____

_____

*Consider getting help and support through
registering at: workshops@crushedtosparkle.com
in the subject title add*
PUTTING MY DREAMS ON HOLD WORKSHOPS.

Chapter 7

FAST TRACK:
Are you a Carer?

Broken Relationships—Are you a Carer?

How did you feel when you received the news that the person you loved or looked up to now totally depends on you?

What I will share with you is simple; however, it is not easy as it requires conscious effort and continuous practice! For me, it is work in progress!

As a carer, do you feel invisible? Do you feel guilty, angry, frustrated, sad, suicidal? Look, I am keeping this very real! This is all about carers looking after others who usually have to put their life on hold, indefinitely!

It is normal to feel sad, angry, isolated, frustrated, or even burdened. Why? Because you are a living HUMAN being with your own desires and dreams!

As a carer, you may feel that you are compromising your hopes and dreams. That you must not eat, exercise, sleep etc. Are you living this hectic lifestyle?

Why? Because you are living every moment thinking and looking to support the cared for! As a carer, your emotions fluctuate quite erratically; however, remember emotion is simply **energy in motion.**

So, let me ask you this:

1. Are you burnt out, "Drowning or exhausted or functioning and operating on your reserves?

_____

2. Are your surviving, "treading water?"

_____

3. Are you thriving, rising up, rising above your current situation?

_____

4. Are you recharging? Are you aligning and balancing your needs?

_____

Ummm, let us explore each of these emotions a little further, shall we? Let us see what they look like, feel like, think like and how it makes you show up and behave in public and private?

Burnout

This is a very toxic negative emotion; you are usually feeling very tired, sad, empty, exhausted, hopeless, flat and possibly suicidal. You are probably asking yourself the question of "Why me? What did I do to deserve this way of life?"

Listen, my question to you is, "**Why not you?**"

_____

_____

"Who would you like to wish this upon instead?

_____

_____

"Umm, think about that for a moment, how do you feel now?

_____

_____

Surviving

This is also another negative emotion. Here you may feel under threat, annoyed, angry, frustrated, paranoid, envious, jealous, impatient, anxious, fearful, irritable, worried and or defensive.

You may wish to lash out and blame others. You may even dwell in "your own pity party" You may believe no one can be trusted, everyone is using you, or that no one cares about you.

Or you may feel that you are alone and invisible.

Or you may continually "verbally vomit" over anyone who simply asks you: "How are you?" As a result of your response and behaviour, you may find that fewer and fewer people ask you that question!

I understand, it is not your intention to lash out; however, you have so much stored up within, and like a pressure cooker you will eventually explode.

So, what can you do when operating in a survival mode?

_____

_____

Are you a Carer?

Take a moment and appreciate what you do have.

1. Did you do that?

_____

Take a moment and think about something that makes you feel good.

2. Did you do that?

_____

Take a moment and do your breathing exercises.

3. Did you do that?

_____

Take a moment and pray.

4. Did you do that?

_____

Take a moment, read/ watch a motivational video.

5. Did you do that?

_____

Take a moment to rest.

6. Did you do that?

_____

Take a moment to be still.

7. Did you do that?

_____

Take a moment and have something good to eat and drink a glass of water.

8. Did you do that?

_____

Take a moment and move away from the person or thing that is upsetting you.

9. Did you do that?

_____

Take a moment, take a moment, take a moment, as time is precious, this living, breathing moment is precious; breathe, inhale 3, exhale 5 repeat 3 times.

10. Did you do that?

_____

Let us continue.

Thriving

This is a positive emotion; you need to learn to relax, rest, and take comfort in knowing that you will find a solution to everything. This emotion makes you feel you can handle a challenge, so you are confident, optimistic, and engaged in activities with a positive mindset.

You may be eager to make progress.

You may even be astonished at your achievements, despite your challenges.

Are you experiencing happy feelings?

_____

If NO why?

_____

_____

If yes Great....

Are you being proud and stimulated to make a difference to make a positive change?

_____

If NO why?

_____

_____

If yes Great....

Now, you are ready to recharge, get those extra boosters to turbo-charge your life. Ironically, the boosters come from being still, calm, at ease, peaceful, mellow, reflective, serene.

After travelling through these different emotions, write down below exactly how you feel.

_____

_____

_____

_____

_____

_____

WARNING: Double Arrow Syndrome

Double Arrow Syndrome

As carers, we tend to be more on the burnout and surviving emotions and in these zones, we can fall victim to the **"double arrow syndrome"** This is where we are struck by a **"situational arrow"**.

Ok, imagine that you are kneeling and cowed over so that your head is aiming to touch your knees or the floor. Now, also imagine, someone has shot you with an arrow in your back — **"situational arrow"** — eg someone criticising you. That arrow is usually one that you cannot control; however, you then pierce another arrow in your back, and this second arrow is your own **"intentional arrow"** placed in and upon yourself, by YOU!!!

What is my point? Well the **first arrow was PAIN,** a physical, mental emotional pain, whereas your **second arrow was SUFFERING**, self-inflicted and completely optional!!!

What are you saying, Juliyah!? Are you telling me that I am causing my own suffering? Yes! How can that be, you may wonder? Explain yourself Juliyah! I think we beg to differ here. Yes, we may, but at least that has got you thinking how you are dealing with your current situation. Can we agree on that?

Ok, great! Let me ask you now to think of your mind as either:

1. a washing machine, or
2. a fast-moving train

Washing machine mind

What????? Please, just work with me for a moment. Let us say that you saw your mind as a washing machine filled with things just moving round and round, a whirring of endless thoughts/ideas. But remember that thoughts are not facts! However, thoughts can create things!

Fast moving trains in your mind

Now imagine that your mind is filled with fast moving miniature trains, running all around and across your mind — famously called trains of thought.

Your point is???? Mind-full vs Mindful
In both scenarios **your mind is full,** mind full, as opposed to being mindful.

Being mindful is being in the moment, being present, focusing on the here and now and nothing else.

Are you a Carer?

In a mindful state, you are free from clutter. You are able to slow down your automatic thoughts on how you read a situation. Being in a mindful state means that you are living in the here and now, being present to what you are actually doing right now.

You are not thinking about past experience or early life experience. You are just focusing on what is happening right here, right now; for example, you are washing the plates, your feel the soapy water on your hands, you examine that the plates are clean, you are NOT thinking about what someone has done to you!

Do you understand?

Mindful is simply being in the present, not thinking about the past or the future, just this moment and what you are doing in it.

Thoughts are not facts; you CAN create new thoughts. So stop procrastinating and be MINDFUL not MIND FULL, my friend xxx

Reflective Notes

Chapter 8

FAST TRACK:
Facing Procrastination

FACING PROCRASTINATION

Procrastination, loosely translated from an etymology dictionary means to go forward, in a slow, sluggish action: **Pro** to go forward, **Crass,** Slow sluggish **Action.**

-Procrastination is self-sabotage, self-destruction. So, stop blaming and complaining but start believing in yourself!!! Come now, get out of your comfort zone and seek ways to improve! Please have an abundance mentality and stretch your thinking as you are inherently a creative being.

Did you know that procrastination is literally squandering time? However, always remember that time just marches on and on. So, if you do not use your time wisely, you will lose time. PLEASE NOTE: time is all we have. This moment, this day, this year will never come back again, so time is what life is made of.

Procrastination is a form of complaining. Please understand and listen, **complaining is not equivalent**

to working! Working means "doing" what are you doing about transforming your life right now? No, I did not say what are others doing for you to transform your life right now! I asked you, "What are your doing right now to transform **your** life?"

Can you see that you have to take personal responsibility to transform your life. Yes, you may get some help along the way; however, do not be complacent and expect others to do the whole work for you in your own life. To think and believe that is upmost selfishness! I believe such expectations place additional burden on others and that's unfair.

Listen, you really need to think about what you want in your life. Why should others stop living their lives in order to build your life?

_____

What is the point or value in that?

_____

Think about value for a second.

How much do you value and respect yourself?

_____

Facing Procrastination

How do you value and respect other's time?

_____

_____

_____

_____

Stop talking yourself out of taking action!

Do change the film running in your mind.

Stop demeaning and devaluing yourself, you are
AMAZING!!!

Believe that!!

Start saying and believing:

I deserve the best!

I deserve the best that life can offer!

I can do... I will do...I must do...

Why? Because I deserve it!

So, believe in yourself as I believe in you xxx

Procrastination

Procrastinating is simply putting off what you should be doing today for some other day. It is intentionally delaying what you know you should be doing.

Listen, I know that procrastination is stopping you from moving forward into your amazing life. Your procrastination is being fuelled by distractions and excuses. You have allowed the media to get inside your head, bombarding you with so much information, but a lot of it could be filtered out. You could take in only what you need in order to move your life forward.

Did you know **procrastination makes you a puppet** and someone else is pulling your stings and they are in control of your life, not you. You have become complacent and comfortable waiting for someone to find the answer for you, for someone to come and rescue you. I am sorry to inform you that YOU are your rescue party! You have the solution to address YOUR LIFE challenges.

Think about that!

Please understand that you are simply just living on someone else's expectation of you!

Facing Procrastination

How does that make you feel? Good? Strong? Happy?

Ummm, so if you are allowing someone else to dictate and determine your life, why are you complaining that your life is not the way it should be. How can it be if you are not taking ownership of your life!

So, let me ask you another question. How would you describe your mindset is it, one of wealth or poverty?

Let us have a look at this.

Wealthy people are usually energetic, happy, doing things they love, doing things for the "greater good", finding solutions etc.

Whereas poverty mindset people usually complain, lack enthusiasm, wallow in self-pity, think about problems. It could be argued that poverty mindset people are selfish as their current state of thinking does nothing to help themselves or others!

FACING PROCRASTINATION

OK, I realise some of you may be offended to be described as having a poverty mindset, but understand procrastination is a poverty, non-creative, non-innovative way to create the life your desire.

So PLEASE make a conscious decision to stop sleepwalking through your life. Please wake up and take action now!

Go ahead and fulfil your promises and dreams you have for yourself.

Listen you are an A* Star performer, your heart is in the right place. Just find your balance!

Consider, getting help and support through registering at:
workshops@crushedtosparkle.com
in the subject title add:
FACING PROCRASTINATION WORKSHOPS.

Chapter 9

Bonus Gift:
Facing the Challenge of Letting Go

FACING THE CHALLENGE OF LETTING GO

Your inner power of letting go - Part 1 of a series

All too often you may have heard people say, "Oh just let it go", "You need to move on" I wondered HOW? Yes, it is easier said than done, but how do you do it? After all, by letting go, you can set yourself free.

So, let us explore how to let go and ensure that we realign and get our mind, body and spirit in sync as opposed to being out of balance.

Evidently, being out of balance sets up the perfect environment to **cause dis ease within the body**, which can result in pain and suffering or erratic emotional behaviours. For example, one minute you are angry and then sad. Then you seek to justify your behaviour to yourself and more than likely crave for some form of addiction or attachment. This is a temporary "fix" to fill the void, e.g. to smoke, take drugs, drink in excess, being promiscuous (to find love, to fill in an empty space in your life). Or you reach out for that cake, overindulge in chocolate or whatever your addiction may be!

However, this relief is very short-lived and you more than likely feel worse afterwards!

Listen, I am just keeping it real, as I have overindulged in chocolate to numb a pain!

Have you ever then blamed the world for your current situation and that no one understands? Do you then succumb into a victim mentality, e.g. that the world is against you, that life is not fair, and question why these things keep happening to you? (Who else would you suggest, if not you?)

So how do you, as En Vogue would say: **"free your mind, and the rest will follow"** My suggestion is to start from within. Consider creating a stillness within and finding a quiet place, then gently say: "**I am at peace, I am a being of peace, I am a soul, I am connected fully to an infinite source of energy.**" The more you repeat this slowly and wrap it up meaningfully with loving emotion, remember, e- motions means energy in motion (e-motion)

Facing the Challenge of Letting Go

Hold on, hold on, wait a minute Juliyah, you are not getting my plight, Juliyah, this is a deep situation that I am currently in, what you are saying is far too simple and to "airy fairy", or just too spiritual for me!

OK, I hear what you say, but just go along with me on this one. As you are fully aware, your current approach to resolving this matter has not provided you with the expected outcome thus far, has it?

So please, be open to change. Be open to open your heart, mind and body. Be open to do something different with loving and emotional intent. By doing so, this can help you heal and work towards becoming more healthy, whole and complete!

Please just stop, think, listen and then take action, slow down your life. Appreciate the present moment, be in the NOW. Be in the here and now, as my late, great godmother Mabel James used to say: "Don't give up, get up, if you fall down, pick yourself up and dust yourself off and keep moving forward, onwards and upwards". She lived to be 99 years old!

Chapter 9: Activity

Remove distractions, create a quiet space, switch off mobile devices

1. Be still, sit or lie down
2. Breathe, concentrate on your breathing in source energy and breathing out your suffering
3. Locate the emotions in your body as you breathe
4. Thank your body for the warning signs
5. Shake, cry, dance, stretch release
6. Take note of anything new you have learnt about yourself
7. Take positive action and start loving yourself unconditionally

Did you do that?

_____

If NO why?

_____

_____

If yes Great....

Facing the Challenge of Letting Go

By not letting go, you are self-sabotaging yourself, and by doing so entering into a vicious cycle which, if left unchecked, could result in your early demise.

As my mentor, Les Brown always says, **"You have greatness in you"**

Or as my other mentor Vishal Marjoria explained the importance of spiritual law and ensuring that all open communication loops must be closed where there is a "**start there must be a finish to create balance once more, alignment and order. `If there are several communication loops open, i.e. unfinished issues, these open communication loops create an environment of chaos to rule your life without order, thus manifesting into several attachment issues**.

So, what will you do next?

_____

_____

Consider getting help and support through registering at:
workshops@crushedtosparkle.com
in the subject title add:
LETTING GO WORKSHOPS.

Reflective Notes

Chapter 10

Bonus Gift:
Summary Les Brown Speaks on Getting UNSTUCK

FACING THE CHALLENGE OF LETTING GO—
SUMMARY LES BROWN "SPEAKS"

Summary of Les Brown, "Getting UNSTUCK"

Juliyah's personal reflection on getting unstuck

This video really allowed me to release so much tension from within. It has truly helped me forgive myself, love myself and forgive others for hurting me.

After all, none of us are perfect and we all need others to forgive ourselves for some past misdemeanours. We now have to forgive them—do not wait for their forgiveness, forgive them now, How?

Write a them a letter expressing your feelings and burn it afterwards! Or why not roleplay and imagine they are in front of you and you tell them how you are feeling and, then swap positions for them to tell you how they feel. Those are 2 strategies to get you started!

Listen, I know it is hard, it is difficult and you may say, well you don't know what X, Y, Z has done to me. And you are right, I do not know what X, Y, Z did to you. However, I do know that life is not fair!

However, are you being fair to yourself? Are you imprisoning yourself in a sea of pity, negativity, anger, despair? So why not try a different, more empowering approach?

What empowering approach? An approach where you are moving from bitter to better. From better to being the best. From your best seek to continually improve yourself, through self-monitoring and self-discipline.

This practice, this process, will allow you to come up with new ways of doing and saying things and your life will never be the same again.

I hope if you are open to it, it will enable you to release and realise your greatness, for you to show up, speak up, stand up and RISE UP into your greatness! Into your POWER!

Over to you, Les Brown

"Forgive and let go, clear your mind of unnecessary baggage, which, weigh you down. What s/he did to me and how bad s/he made me feel, how that person, made you so, angry.

Forgiveness, this is a conscious deliberate effort, focus on developing myself, move and grow, get on, what am I going to do now... stop the victim mentality, stop repeating the story, over and over again and over again to anyone who cared to listen. Stop it, do you know, everybody has a story, 80% of people don't care about your story and 20% are happy that is happening to you and not them! All of us have story to tell.

Listen, in life we will have tragedy, now tragedy will destroy your life, or you can create from this. Know that you are bigger than the problem, you need to, declare, all-out war on that issue, know that that you will get out of this rut.

Listen, Murphy's law, will happen, anything can happen, there are different seasons and sometimes, you just do not want to even get out of bed, sometimes you are in a slum mood and you do not even know why.

Listen, just continue to execute, stay busy, work your plan, evaluate yourself. Look, consider a bow and arrow, in order to take aim, you have to pull back to a point and then release, listen, pray, mediate, go on holiday and recharge your battery.

Learn to discipline your emotions or they will run your life in default mode.

Consider your mind as fertile ground, remove the weeds, it is a process and requires procedures to go through. Do self-monitor to avoid: default modes of revenge. Which is, loaded with guilt, replace those debilitating modes of thinking with personal: greatness, being happy, being successful and having a happy life, in spite of this/these challenge(s).

Say to yourself: I am in control of this, I am not going to let it destroy me. I will rise up, I come back to fulfil my dreams, health and peace of mind. I am going to do something about this situation.

Listen, expect it to get better, this event will come to pass, it is not here to stay, put life in perspective, evaluate yourself.

Personal dynamics, both individually and collectively. Say with me: "where there is always a will, there is a way, I am unstoppable! This will not get me down."

Know that you will have low moments, however, create and have high lows do things for yourself, pray, go for that walk in the park, rest, listen to upbeat music, exercise, read motivational books, watch motivational videos take full responsibility of your life.

Accept where I am, I accept conditions as they exist or I will take full responsibility to change them, I got me here, I am not a volunteer victim.

Did you know that there are 3 types of people

1. *Make things happen*
2. *Watch what happens and*
3. *Not sure what is happening.*

I have decided to decide, and change my strategy and recreate me. I will change my life. I will stand up to life. I will live each day as if it was my last. I will work on myself and develop me and empower me.

That was then, this is now. That is what I did then, and I am in charge. I can't change the past; however, I can recreate how interpret the past and it empowers me. I will love myself unconditionally and I forgive myself. If I knew better, I would have done better.

Within my mind's eye, I forgive myself unconditionally. I let go, and if I want to be forgiven, I forgive others. I throw away any negativity that has been holding me back.

Practice makes improvement. Better your best, be bigger than what you do. Take on new practices, new breakthroughs. Things will happen to me on the blind side, knock me down. However, they will not knock me out. I will have a fast recovery; I will keep empowering company. I will make myself feel good about the process of transforming. I will listen to motivational resources.

What is life?

1. *Getting unstuck means… living through life on my terms not gliding on life every day on automatic.*

2. *I am aware of special powers within and excited about my unfolding future, as I know that things will get better,*

3. *I will cry,*

4. *Life will take me to my knees, but the pains, these pains will open spaces in my heart for joy.*

   a) *Life is like an onion, unpeel one layer at a time and sometimes… cry.*

   b) *Life is a challenge, meet it as a gift, accept it adventure it, dare it, have sorrows with it. Overcome it… life is tragedy face it,*

c) *Life is duty, perform it.*

d) *Life is a game, play it.*

e) *Life is a mystery, unfold it.*

f) *Life is a song, so sing it.*

g) *Life is an opportunity, so take it.*

h) *Life is a journey, so complete it.*

i) *Life is a promise, so fulfil it.*

j) *Life is a beauty, so praise it, enjoy it.*

k) *Life is a struggle, fight it.*

l) *Life is a goal, achieve it.*

m) *Life is a puzzle, solve it."*

Les Brown

Chapter 10 Activity

Over to you......

Now tell me how you feel about both reading and watching Les Brown?

_____

_____

_____

_____

_____

How has this impacted your life?

_____

_____

_____

_____

_____

Summary Les Brown Speaks on Getting UNSTUCK

What will you do next to move your life forward?

_____

_____

_____

_____

_____

_____

Would you like to connect with Les Brown?

_____

*Consider getting help and support through
registering at: workshops@crushedtosparkle.com
in the subject title add:
GETTING UNSTUCK LES BROWN
CONNECTIONS WORKSHOPS.*

Crushed to Sparkle

Thank you for....

Being so open and honest about

Your personal

And professional growth

And development

As a reward

I would love to give you a few

"MAGIC KEYS"

Chapter 11

JULIYAH'S "MAGIC" KEYS

JULIYAH'S GOLDEN KEYS

1. Tap into your personal and professional power. How? By minding your own business and getting your life on track and not being forced into another person's track in which they control your pace!

2. Healthy and Wealthy—Review your lifestyle; make a habit to be the best version of yourself. Consider becoming an independent health and wellbeing business owner working from home with and International Licence to sell health and wellbeing products in over 160 Countries, for more life changing information go straight to:

   www.queenangelcreations.com/Forever

3. Healthy and wealthy—Learn to make money from your smart phone for more information go to:

   www.befactor.com

   contact **Juliyah@CrushedtoSparkle.com**,
   email title write **BE Wealthy**.

4. Know that you will stumble, fall and make mistakes; however, GET UP, DUST YOURSELF DOWN, LICK YOUR WOUNDS AND MOVE FORWARD. You cannot change the past — you can only optimise this present moment, which will then sow the seeds of change to harvest your future for tomorrow.

5. Create and seek synergistic alliances, simply collaborate.

6. Create a mindset of positive change and abundance; there is more than enough for all of us to live an abundant life.

7. Strive towards unity and respect diversity.

8. Understand that each one can teach one and together we can all learn, develop and grow.

9. Be creative — create **"your magic"**, be innovative, solution-oriented and have FUN, LAUGH, care to share. IMAGINE and know that you have the power to fuse, blend and create newness!

10. Share the love, show kindness and empathy, have a **"human touch"** a simple goodwill gesture could easily save someone's life. Try smiling more as that may just give a person more of an extra mile to carry on when they were ready just to give up. A word at the right time could uplift someone with

suicidal thoughts. Please do carry out random acts of kindness.

11. Find solutions and you will overcome adversity; you know that you cannot please everyone, so stop trying to!!! Doing so is a quick way to cause imbalance in all aspects of your life.

12. Invest in yourself, in your education, training and development. Consider getting help and support through registering at: workshops@ crushedtosparkle.com in the subject title add: BE YOUR OWN AUTHOR ARCHITECT AND ARTIST OF YOUR LIFE WORKSHOPS.

JULIYAH'S PLATINUM KEYS

Now that you have read and completed the self-discovery toolkit within this book from cover to cover, please consider doing the following...

Action Steps.

1. Reflect on how you feel.

2. How do you look?

3. Look at your before and after pictures

4. Re-read your over to you and activity sections in each chapter.

5. Complete the online evaluation form

6. Please submit a testimonial

7. Please, would you be so kind as to provide company details of a company that you know that this book could help their staff?

8. Who could you suggest would benefit from Crushed to Sparkle (C2S) course? As a thank you for caring to share you will get a free book and a Discount voucher for C2S courses.

9. Register your interest for the next workshop in your country.

10. Meditate and practice Mindfulness

11. Please go to the park, or nature's garden...just spend time in nature and be at one with nature.

12. Be creative, innovative and optimistic

13. Be proactive in transforming complex challenges or issues and reduce them into simple actionable tasks

14. Take off the brakes or blinders and move from STOP to GO,

15. Now is your time to think beyond the status quo and create a new standard

16. Now, plan your own definition of success

17. Observe the changes: Look NOW on how you see, feel, look about yourself,

18. Be aware of how others are treating you now

19. Notice how much or little impact other people's opinions have on you now.

20. The way forward is to observe, assess, plan and implement the plan, then evaluate and review

21. **Love and Live each day on purpose**

22. If you want to treat yourself or others to a bespoke gift, for example to say: "I love you," "congratulations" "miss you", "sorry". Happy 13th 16th 18th or baby shower gifts or floral arrangements for birth, marriage or death, then I will kindly invite you to visit: **www.queenangelcreations.com**, where we "Gift a piece of happiness"

Reflective Notes

_____

_____

_____

_____

_____

_____

_____

_____

_____

_____

_____

_____

_____

_____

Chapter 12

EXTRA BOOSTERS FOR YOU!

Develop the following building blocks:

1. Mentally — unstoppable strength

2. Spiritual — life filled with faith

3. Financial — Freedom

4. Entrepreneurial — Enterprising spirit

5. Powerful and positive outlook on your life

6. Creative and innovative problem-solving skills

7. Physical flexibility and engaging presence

8. Nurturing — temperament, seeing the best in others even when others do you wrong

9. RISE UP — Stand for something, speak out, show up and shine through the challenges; after all, you are phenomenal!!!

Crushed to Sparkle

As you go along your life journey, say to yourself:

1. I am getting lighter and brighter,
2. I can soar,
3. I can flow,
4. I can adapt to any environment
5. I am a phenomenal human being
6. I am an Enlightened Warrior, King/Queen
7. I can create magic, simply because I can imagine!

Know that you are AMAZING inside and out, dream big and then bigger still!

Final homework activity

Please honestly complete

I AM _____

_____

I CAN _____

_____

I WILL _____

_____

I MUST _____

_____

Now my dear friend, honour what you have written above, be your own very best friend, chairwoman, Chairman and LOVE yourself first, this is not being selfish, as you can only give what you have got. So fuel, fill, empower, encourage yourself until you OVERFLOW. Now you are in a much more powerful position to give and help others.

So I encourage you to, Live, Laugh, Love, Light up this world with your good positive vibrations self. Be that change that makes the world of difference!

Reflective Notes

_____

_____

_____

_____

_____

_____

_____

_____

_____

_____

VIP PRAYERS

CARE TO SHARE A PRAYER: PSALM 23

Lets discuss the verse and then the action

The Lord is my shepherd, *Living in action, my interpretation in brackets)

<u>*Verse 1*</u> *The Lord is my shepherd, I shall not want*
(You are not alone)

<u>*Verse 2*</u> *He maketh me to lie down in green pastures: He leadeth me beside the still waters.*
(Rest Be open to be guided to a better place)

<u>*Verse 3*</u> *He restoreth my soul He leadeth me in the paths of righteousness for his name's sake*
(You are healthy, whole and complete. Be open to listen and obey to THE MOST HIGH GOD)

<u>*Verse 4*</u> *Yea, though I walk through the valley of the shadow of death, I will fear no evil: for Thou art with me: thy rod and they staff they comfort me.*

(Face your challenges, be not afraid the THE MOST is with you and will provide you with resources to get you through it, HAVE FAITH)

<u>Verse 5</u> *Thou preparest a table before me in the presence of mine enemies;* (Yes there will always be people who do not wish you well, however, trust in the Lord as he prepares for your greateness to manifest in the presence of those who had negative intentions towards you)

Thou annointeth my head with oil; my cup runneth over. (The Most High, will cleanse, oil you and provide you with ABUNDANCE)

<u>Verse 6</u> *Surely goodness and mercy shall follow me all the days of my life: and I will dwell in the house of the LORD for ever.* (The MOST HIGH will proved total protection for you life)

Proverbs 3:5-6

"Trust in the Lord, with all your heart and lean not on your own understanding. In all your ways acknowledge him, and he will make your crooked paths straight"

Juliyah's prayer for you

As I say these words in faith, that you the creator of all there is, will guide, nurture, support, and maintain and sustain me. Lord, God, you know that I stumble, I fall, I do say unkind things and think unclean thoughts, help bathe me from the inside out.

My words are so limited to express and convey your illuminating magnificence. All I can say is thank you, thank you, thank you, I give you all thanks and praises to see through another day; thank you for my health and strength.

Lord, teach me how to follow your ways, and do right. Lord, show me what it is that you want me to do for you today. I am your humble servant. I love you Lord, I need you Lord. When others fail me Lord, you are always there, in both the good and the bad times. Your love is unfailing.

Lord, forgive me when I get angry with you, simply because it appears to me that even though I fast, pray, meditate, give to charity, things do not seem to be shifting for the better in my life.

Lord help me to have an attitude of gratitude, whilst I am waiting, waiting for my moment. Help me, to be patient and not get angry over such little things. Help me show love and appreciation to myself and others.

Crushed to Sparkle

Lord, help me do something today both anonymously and publicly for another and not expect anything from them in return. Let me learn to practice what I preach about abundant mentality, as there is more than enough for everyone.

Mother of creation, thank you for our planet earth and the universe, help us to respect and work with nature and not rape and ravish nature.

Mother of creation, help us to be at one with nature, to see the rhythm and dance of life, let us work collaboratively, let us co-operate to make the world a much better world, let us heal the world; however, mother of creation we have to heal ourselves first. Help us do this and for us to do this well.

Heavenly parents, please heal us from the inside out. Bathe each cell within our body. Teach us how to love, realign and set our internal frequencies and vibrations to ensure balance inside, so we can manifest balance on the outside.

Lord, please soften our harden hearts, remove the scales from our eyes, remove the vile off our tongues and reduce our egos, for in the grand scale of things, unity is community, so let us build up one another and not to destroy one another.

Lord help us to ask ourselves the question. What is the benefit in destruction? It will only cause perpetual pain and suffering. Let us heal, let us work in balance, let us work in peace. Let God's love show up and shine out in each and every one of us.

Let us fulfill the greatest tenet of any faith-based person and that is spread the love xxx

God, I release all my concerns into your loving care, I will wait on the Lord of which is my everything, my all and all.

Thank you, Thank you, Thank you.

Amen, Amen, Amen xxx

Final Activity

Over to you, now you create your own heartfelt prayer below, better still **write your prayer on a separate card or on a paper**, so that you can read it daily to feed you mind, body and soul xxx

Reflective Notes

_____

_____

_____

_____

_____

_____

_____

_____

_____

_____

_____

_____

Printed in Great Britain
by Amazon

25068361R00109